HAVING LOVED

Having Loved

new poems

by Judith Malina

Fast Books

Cover image: "Loki" by Julian Beck
Drawings by Judith Malina

Copyright © 2015 by Judith Malina

ISBN 978-0-9887162-5-4

Fast Books are edited and published by Michael Smith, P. O. Box 1268, Silverton, OR 97381, USA

Contents

Time Travel	1
Mirrors of Memory	2
Beyond Number	3
Birth of the Body	4
Watching the News	5
Fatal Flaw	6
My Story	7
The Birdcage	8
Haiku	9
What Matters	10
Following Artaud	11
Chestnuts in Wartime	12
Funny	13
Ripening	14
Overcoming Pain	16
Rats, Always	17
The Splendor Shines	18
Awaiting the Messiah	19
The Evil Inclination	20
After Midnight	21
The End	22
Regrets Pile Up	23
Half the World at War	24
To Hear, To See, To Know	25
Mabel Beck	26
We Call It Holy	27
Let Me Go	28
Roma	29
Approaching the Flame	30
The Women of Iraq	31
The Shortcoming of Poetry	32
In the Movies	33
Dark Truth	34

Heavy	35
Wicker	36
The Soul Soars	37
The Gods of Greece	39
Time Seems to Pass More Quickly As One Grows Old	40
The Fruit of the Action	41
And Be No Dream	42
The Ultimate Eye	43
Like It Is	44
On My Deafness	45
How It Could Be Otherwise	46
Who Will Hear?	47
In Silence	48
Before I Forget	49
My Peanuts	50
Rage and Blame	51
The Resister	52
Flushing	53
The Bridge	55
Consolation	56
Too Soon	57
Collision	58
Sparks and Flashes	59
The Perpetrators of the Law	60
Slipping Down	61
To Poetry	63
Jerusalem	64
For Tuli Kupferberg	65
Radiation Poems	66
Asking Too Much	68
The Power of Love	69
The Bed of Suffering	70
Loki	71
Truth	72

Your World	73
The Perfection	74
Flying	75
Huyler's Trail	76
On Hearing the Terrible News	77
Talking to Myself	78
Resting My Eyes	79
The Survivor	80
First Step	81
The Bird Flies	82
I Grieve	83
Time	84
Watching the Sky	85
Faithful Practice	87
The Bird	88
Justice	89
Tides	90
Weaving	91
Discourse	92
As If	93
Now That I Am Home	94
Sunset	95
No, No, No, No, No	96
All the Way	97
Hard Lessons	98

Time Travel

Sweeping across Italy
As the players have always done
Since remembered time
Roads built for troops of soldiers
Traversed by troubadours and troupes
Of the Commedia who saw
From their windows
Or the back of the caravan
Much the same scenery,
Except for the paved road
And the telephone wires,
Seeing sunset and hurrying to reach
Orvieto before the twilight.

Mirrors of Memory

When I was happy I thought I was sad
And now I am sad remembering
How I once was happy. Mirrored illusions
Infect my memory, displacing perspective
With nostalgic distortions
That are nobody's fault.

Beyond Number

What can be counted is nothing.
What counts is beyond numbering.

BIRTH OF THE BODY

I will forge the head of Zeus
Out of the body of Minerva
And the labor, yes, the labor,
Is the pain that brings to birth
The hard-headed men
From the soft-hearted women's wombs
When wisdom sprang full-bodied,
Yes, full-bodied, from his brain
And the curses of the muses
Wept and constructed an anvil
Of flesh and metal and music
To forge out of man's head
The body of wisdom.

Watching the News

I am watching for the insight
That will make me shout
"Eureka!"
There is only news of wars
And catastrophes. And if there's a trumpet
I haven't heard it yet.
But I try to stay attentive.
The rest of the channels
Ring with hymns of stupidity
To make us laugh, to make bearable the news
Of wars and catastrophes.

Fatal Flaw

Death, that fatal side effect
Of life, spoils everything
With its unhappy ending.

My Story

I live on an island
In the Atlantic Ocean
Close to the coast of
North America's mainland.

The island is densely inhabited
And some of its inhabitants
Feel themselves part
Of social and ethnic neighborhoods.

I grew up in a bilingual
German Jewish community.
My father was the Rabbi
Of the German Jewish Congregation.
My mother was ambitious
And trained me to my art.

My father's death
Was her abiding tragedy.
I grew up in her grief
And I still have a heavy heart.

Most people who live on this island
Have a heavy heart
Though cheerfulness is considered
A mandatory virtue.

The Birdcage

She opened the door
Of the birdcage.
"Time will save itself,"
She said, "It makes
Its own conditions."

The bird flew several times
Around the room
Before it found the window.
"We don't really know
What time is," she whispered
As she closed the door
Of the empty birdcage.

Haiku

When I draw these lines
Across the yellowing page
I am studying

What Matters

Never put off a poem
Not for an instant
Lest it perish like
The wisp of
A dream,
Lost.

Let the person from Porlock
Knock without answering …
His message
Doesn't matter.
The poem
Does.

Following Artaud

Listening to Artaud
At the Scholars' Conference:
They talk sanely
Of madness. I pretend
To be sane
But I am demented
Like our hero.

Following Artaud
Into the forbidden theatre
Where he lost himself
In madness,
I strive for the infinite
Possibilities
Like the insane.

Chestnuts in Wartime

I cook chestnuts in various forms
Sometimes I am political
And sometimes I am non-political

I gather chestnuts, I roast them,
I bake them, I cook them,
I grind them into flour.
I make chestnut soups, pureés, jams,
I mix them with whatever is
Available: what grows in the ground
By the riverbed, onions and berries.
Sometimes I am part of the war,
Sometimes I think I am the only
Sane person on the battlefield.

There is only one road to Rocchetta
And not many provisions
Come through in these times. And we
Between the torrents of the Sisola and the Borbera,
We eat chestnuts in all forms.

Funny

Stepped on the line.
Not a word. Not a word.
That's how one knows it's serious.
Learned everything from early cinema.
The hills are still green
But autumn leaves will change all that.
And either the rage will subside
Or there'll be a shift in lifestyle.

Funny about the future,
How it's both the next few minutes
And the long haul into eternity.

Ripening

I was a poet then
And all things glistened
With a thousand exclamations!
Now I am content to make
A sentence with a single clause.

Overcoming Pain

Come,
Spend some time with me
Perhaps there's something I can tell you
That you don't yet know.
Or something you can tell me
That I need to know.
I am plowing through the murk
Of my condition,
I am eating the bread of affliction.
You cannot imagine
The tremor or the joy of it,
I mean of understanding the pain
And overcoming it.

Rats, Always

Was it ever, ever pure,
This building of the haven
Of faith and grandeur
In the barbaric wilderness?
Was the classical facade
Always and only
A façade—and the rats
Always there underneath?

The Splendor Shines

The splendor
Shines
Splintering
The sparks
Shattering
The formations

Awaiting the Messiah

Why am I looking in the news?
Why do I turn every hour
To hear or see what they say
Has happened?

I am awaiting the Messiah.
I am listening for the answer.
I am searching for a clue.
I am Kandinsky standing
In front of Monet's haystack
About to discover a simple
Truth that changes everything.

The Evil Inclination

From the time that Eve
Put her ear to the serpent
And was thrilled
By the evil inclination
To this morning's quarrel,
When she said the most hurtful
Words that she could think of
To show him how she suffers,
There has been no peace
In the house
Or in the region
Or in the whole wide world.

Yet it is given to us
To stop repeating
This …

After Midnight

The day begins in the night,
It always has, the day
Begins in the night, the day
Which is always bright
Begins in the dark.
Children find it hard to believe
In the mystique of midnight,
That after the midnight hour
It's tomorrow. Tomorrow begins
In the night, it always has …

The End

Nothing is endless
Not even suffering
Though it may seem so
To the sufferer.
Take heart: the end
Is in sight.

Regrets Pile Up

You let go
Thinking the time will come
But then they die
And the time will not come
And then regrets pile up
On top of us
And smother everything

Half the World at War

Is it ever really over, the war?
Or does it only change shapes and names?

When I was a little child I asked,
"When was the first war?"
"When Cain killed Abel," said my mother.
"But that wasn't a war.
That was only two people."
"There were only four people.
It was half the world."

To Hear, To See, To Know

Tinnitus rings
Through the silent falling snow.
It's been years since I've heard
Even a moment of silence.
But I see the snow
And I know …

Mabel Beck

I think of Mabel standing
Here, remembering Irving
Going to work every morning,
Remembering Franklin and Julian
Going to school every morning ...

I remember her remembering,
Standing at this same window.
And now we have sold the place,
And Isha will not stand at this window
Remembering how I remembered
Julian, in a tuxedo
Hailing a cab ...

WE CALL IT HOLY

Every moment reveals again
The great nothingness.
And then there is the Shabbat,
Which bears the distinction
Of not being part of the nothingness.
Which is why we call it holy
And keep it apart from the week.

LET ME GO

Let me go now as I came,
With a great cry and a great hope.

ROMA

This city is the ruin
Of ancient Rome's empire
As New York is the ruin
of the wigwams of the Algonquin.
Wherever we go we step on the past,
On the graves of our ancestors,
On the graves of our mothers.
Every apple is the fruit
Of the soil out of which it grew.
And I bite the past
With my teeth,
And my feet tread on the remnants
Of the belovéd buried
In the mass graves
Of our bloody history.

Approaching the Flame

I have no courage.
Let me "go forth" as a coward
Scared to death in my heart
As I approach the flame,
While my brave feet
Carry me forward,
And I am glad to serve
The best and not the worst in me.

The Women of Iraq

O women of Iraq
Under the bombs of the navy
Of my adopted country,
I feel my solidarity
And my sisterhood with you,
In your black capes and hoods
Making life out of rubble.

I hear the morning's news.
American soldiers are eating
The gazelles of their enemies.
I have no enemies. I declare my kinship
With the women of Iraq who, like me,
Don't eat the pig,
Who pray as I do
To the one God who mourned the belovéd
Under the rubble,
And I make, in your name,
The petition that I may never,
God willing, eat a gazelle.

The Shortcoming of Poetry

The bay is wide. The colors
Come up before the sun rises.
The spirit cowers before the sunrise,
Exorcising the unbearable beauty
With "Ah! That's lovely," crying out
Again the impossible
That for all our poetry is mute
In the face of grandeur, holiness, and love.

In the Movies

In the movies
The finished product
Is always the Ultimate Lie.
The truth is on the set,
Where we conspire,
Sometimes hundreds of us,
To make them believe
In the fiction we are weaving.

Sometimes thousands of them,
Sometimes millions believe us,
And we believe too
That we are realizing
The fiction. The fiction
Of our hopes and fears,
Realizing them to make it real.
More real than the hunger
Of the poor, or the horror
Of the rich.
To make it like Vesuvius,
Looming above us
For good or for evil,
A threatening mountain
Signaling the eternal
In the moment. We know
On the set
That God's camera
Is always running, and this
Is the only take.

Dark Truth

You comfort me
Like a forest on wheels.
I open my arms, but my hands
Have been cut off by the wind.
Were I a scarecrow, the birds
Would fly from me. But look!
I am an acorn
Feeling the oak inside me.
No, the forest is running
And I run after it
Calling your name.

Heavy

The sun on my back
Stones in my heart
The heavy weight
Of hopes
Unfulfilled and now
Unfulfillable
That weigh me down

WICKER

I look up at the sunlight
Through the trees
As innocently as when I first saw it
From my wicker carriage.
I remember the wicker particularly
Because I slept on a wicker couch
In the hospital waiting room
When my mother woke me to say
They had done everything they could
But my father was dead.
After that nothing made sense.
So I became a Surrealist …
The wicker woven through my tears …
And snow, in my old age, when it's all
Clear: that it never could make sense.
I look at the sunlight
Through the leaves
As innocently …

The Soul Soars

Can't speak
My mouth is full of mud—
Or is it blood?
Can't see
My eyes, not dazzled
But dry as sand.
Can't write
My hands tremble and won't
Follow thoughts.
But still the soul
Soars above
And won't be still
Till I am.

THE GODS OF GREECE

The great Hellenic vision of divinity
Whose taint is present
In our Hebrew faith
When we say Lord—
As if God were
Some earthly master.

God wove sorrow
Into the fabric
Of our being
When God
Made us mortal.

TIME SEEMS TO PASS MORE QUICKLY AS ONE GROWS OLD

The hours are like minutes now,
The days like hours.
Still the nights are long.

The weeks are like days now,
The months like weeks.
Still the nights are long.

The years are like months now.
Still ...

The Fruit of the Action

The joy is in the doing
Not in the having done.
And yet while we are doing
We think only of the goal.
This is the fruit of the action
Of which Gandhi warned,
Where the move of what is to come
Besmirches the present moment.
Thus wisdom makes a fool of knowledge.
Thus knowledge makes a fool of wisdom.

And Be No Dream

O splendor lost and ever beckoning us
To the vision of the world we want.
O delusion, manifest your power
To make the best come true
And be no dream.

The Ultimate Eye

I will not flinch
To meet the final lover.
I, who have always been afraid
Of everything and no one,
Will look him in his ultimate eye,
And not be afraid.

All my long life I've been afraid
Of water and of wind and of the dark,
Of aloneness and of pain,
Of speed and steep places,
But in the end
I will not flinch
Nor will I laugh in his face
But we will laugh together
Like children playing,
Because now we are safe.

Like It Is

It goes by like a flash of lightning.
A lifetime, I mean.
It's the length of a spark.
You know that nothing you can do
Will change its brevity.
You can meditate your ass off
But you won't stop the course of the minutes.
You can send your mind
Into an illusion of slowness,
And while your mind is floating
In eternity, your body
Is being battered
By the ten thousand hammers of time.
All you can do is be aware of it.

On My Deafness

In the silence
Poetry returns
And fills my brain
With music never heard

How It Could Be Otherwise

It's hard to imagine how it could be otherwise,
The sky grey, the sense of a colorless color repeated
Silently without relief. Every night around this hour
It grows darker, every morning the light comes up again.
Every year passes without a trace
Except in the face and in the spine. Where's the joy
Now, that we seem to remember? Where's
The sweet voice that sang? They just don't
Make them like that anymore. But there could
Be some kid somewhere with a whole new idea.
Let's hope so. Meantime, watch the sky
Grow dark every night around this hour.

WHO WILL HEAR?

Call out, like a creature in a play, "Beware! Beware!"
But who will hear you? The audience
Is fast asleep. The curtain may or may not
Have risen or fallen, or been eliminated
At some other time. "Where am I?" says the person
Waking from a faint. Where are we?
We are waking from a faint.

In Silence

In silence
And in the screaming shrapnel
We hear the angels sing

Before I Forget

There's still so much to do and I'm
Running out of time ...
So I assume the position of spirit
And speed my steps and
The lovely looseness of time
To hurry to say what I have to say
Before I forget.

My Peanuts

The dried fig tree will flower and fruit again.
Look, I am presenting my peanuts
To the elephantine throes of your desire.
Can you cope with that under the canopy
Of the connubial? Don't retreat.
The march forward has much to offer,
Ripe figs and figures of fulfilled aspirations.

Rage and Blame

Oh God you have not forsaken me
But I forsook you
In the despair of my misery.
Instead of saying the Kaddish
To praise, honor, and glorify
I spouted rage and blame
That he who was young should die
And I who am old should live.
Instead of the praise, honor, and glory
I condemned the holy judgment
And cried out at the stench,
Proclaiming the Oneness
Which is my only understanding
Of the continuity of our lives
And the disruption of our death.

The Resister

The resister is always a part of what she resists
By devoting the self to it, by acknowledging it.
I am that part of the capitalist system
That struggles against the principles of interest
And exploitation.
Still I pay cash for my bread.

I am that part of the hierarchical system
That rejects authority
And sees a better way to conduct society.
Still I obey the policeman.

I am that part of the system of violence and punishment
That proposes to eliminate all weapons…

FLUSHING

When I flush
I want to see it go down,
That which was inside me vanishing.
When I was a child
I was afraid of losing
What was just warmly inside
To the dark cold waters.
Now I am glad.

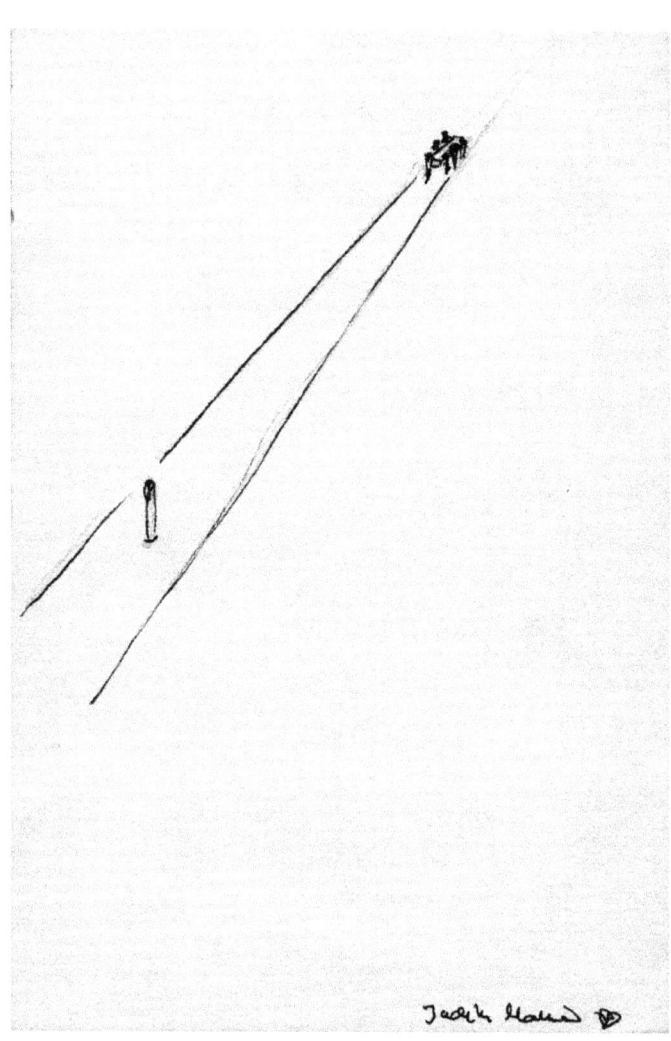

The Bridge

The terrorists express
The desire of the people.
The people don't want terror,
The people want peace and prosperity.
The people also want to get rid of the abuses.
The terrorists express
The desire of the people to get rid of the abuses.

The terrorists blow up the bridge
To get rid of the abuses.
The people want the bridge.
The people want to get rid of the abuses.
The terrorists say, "The bridge
Is part of the abuses."
And the people ask the poets how can we resolve
This contradiction?

Consolation

Don't try to comfort each other,
It only mocks the bereaved.
Allen Ginsberg laughed in my face.
"It's only death!" he cried
At Julian's funeral.
But in a few more years, Allen was dead.
The best message came from Nanda in Milan.
"It's all so stupid," she said.
And that may be all the consolation
We can offer ...

TOO SOON

To what end do we turn out the light?
To what end do we cry for help?
To what end do we wash our hands?
To what end do we die too soon?

For the sake of the birds that still fly
For the sake of remembered love
For the sake of the endless absence
For the sake of the unnameable One

How much of the fruit can we eat?
How much of the weight can we carry?
How much can we give and take?
How much till we choke on the pulp?

As much as we dared to do
As much as we understand
As much as we fail every moment
As much as we can

I have always turned out the light
You have never cried out for help
We always have worked with our hands
They always have died too soon

Collision

The slivers of the universe
Shatter around me.
The multitudinous Zimzum
And the Essential Unity
Have collided in my heart.
My individual cosmos
Is broken. I am only one
Of the vessels that smashed
At the Holy Moment: Now.

Sparks and Flashes

Every moment is the only moment.
We always knew it,
But we don't know how to live it.
We live the fictional continuity
That novels teach us,
That biographies grasp
To exemplify in exemplary lives.
That's not the way it is.
A life of sparks and flashes
Is what we live, luminous moments
Swift as the twinkle
Of the firefly—no story, just a series
Of ellipses.

The Perpetrators of the Law

The perpetrators of the law
Pretend to maintain calm and order
Even though there be no upsurge
Of joyous digressions. Neither
Is there calm and order.

The perpetrators of the law
Separate each of us from the other
By building economic structures,
Of which suffering is the foundation.

The perpetrators of the law
Have created injustice
With heavy tomes of precepts
Incompatible with human needs.

Look, tens of thousands are in the streets now,
Chanting, "We will not
Improve the laws, we will
Abolish them!"

Slipping Down

Slipping down
Into the dreaded infinite,
Into the dark of nothingness,
Into eternal forgetting.
O I am scared
Of the empty space
Into which I am falling.
There is no ground beneath my shoes
And nothing above or below,
Only the sensation of slipping down ...

To Poetry

Nothing to do now
But to commit
The passing instant
To the eternal life
Of poetry.
No time for other
Than this.

Jerusalem

I was reading the Hebrew myths
In the city of Jerusalem
And I fell asleep on the book
And I dreamed that an ancient king
With a golden crown
Rose out of the maps
And asked me, What do you make of these myths?
And I said, Nothing. One myth's enough for me.
And he asked me further,
What do you make of those gods?
And I said, One God is enough for me.
And he asked me, Then why are you crying?
And I said, Because the God of my soul
Is a merciful God, and the God
In the only book is not a merciful God.
But before David under his crown
Could justify God to me, I woke
To the news of wars.

For Tuli Kupferberg

I salute you
Tuli
As a revolutionary
Pioneer
Treading with
Laughing disdain
On all the lines
Of the forbidden,
Making the world
Howl at its vices
And rejoicing
In the infinite
Possibilities.

Radiation Poems

The invisible ray
Pierces my right breast
Penetrating my flesh
Without any sensation
To pinpoint the spot
Where the tumor was
To prevent recurrence.

Punished the innocent
In Hiroshima.

I feel no pain, I feel
The lights flashing
Red and white, and
The click-clacking of the
Machine. Then why?

The mystery of the northern lights
Surged through my breast.

Burnt the pagodas
Of Nagasaki down?

Then the burns came, painful red burns
Under my breast and
My armpit
Stinging pains shoot
Through my flesh

The invisible ray will do
Its best to burn through and through
But though my skin
Like branded cattle
Smarts, I am no beast
But signal through the flames
I cannot see, waiting
In a room of wounded women
Talking of their pain and their doctors
And their medications.

Asking Too Much

I stuffed the universe into my pocket
And made it my notebook.
I wrote in it,
"Total bliss for everyone forever."
And they said,
Isn't that asking too much?
No, it isn't. Not for my notebook.
Not for the universe in my pocket.
Is there another universe?
Not in my pocket.

The Power of Love

Let me remember only the good parts—
Were there others? I don't remember.
I only remember how we were determined
To change the whole world
With our love,
To make it
As loving as we were—
And believe in the power of love
As if it were stronger than all the armies
Because we believed it,
And we were determined.

The Bed of Suffering

Watching the time go by
At the bed of suffering.
Is it too slow or too fast?
The second hand makes its round
From twelve to twelve.
The measured heartbeat and breath
Has its own rhythm,
Sometimes too fast or too slow.
The doctors come and go,
The nurses attend the details
At the bed of suffering.
But the belovéd can only weep
Or refrain from weeping,
Watching the time go by.

Loki

I see a ship.
I see a prison with bars.
I see a stage set ...
I see a palace with columns.
I see a shack in a favela.
I see a small painting
By Julian Beck
Called Loki.

Truth

Blessed be the blasphemous
For they have told us the truth.

Your World

I am a part of the universe
Which you created.
Therefore let me be consoled!
I cannot lose the world,
Because it is yours
And I am part of it.

The Perfection

I can imagine The Perfection,
And though I don't, alas, expect it,
I try to prepare for it as if
The Perfection were about
To walk in the door.

Hello, Perfection, I said joyously.
But it had passed like any moment.
Yet I'll prepare.

Flying

I dreamed that the actors could fly,
Extending the possibilities of the staging.
Our space is small.
They glided under the ceiling,
They hovered over the audience,
They reached their hands to the audience.

Then I dreamed that the audience could fly.
"Time for great street theatre," I thought
As I awakened.

Huyler's Trail

Standing on the banks of the Hudson
On Huyler's Trail with your son
Now grown grey, and older
Than you ever were,
I think of the thousands of others,
Sparks in the darkness of memory,
Lighting with a brief glimmer
What will soon be forgotten.

It is a wickedness of time and nature
That you should not remember me
While I cannot in my lifetime forget you.

If it must be so,
Sayonara.
Farewell.

Who dies first is spared
The anguish of the survivor.
Sayonara.

On Hearing the Terrible News

Everything vanished
Even the light of day
Even the soothing darkness of the night
Even the fear of death
Slipped into nothingness.
Even the nothingness vanished.

Even the suffering of the people
Even the poetry, music, even
The splendor subsided.
Nothing remained,
Not sky nor world nor pleasure nor pain
Nor love …

Talking to Myself

I talk to myself
As if I were someone else.
And I am someone else.
I talk to her.

Resting My Eyes

I rest my eyes
Against the color of the sky
Without considering the depths
That lie beyond: neither
Winged angels, nor
Galactic swirls,
Only the color grey,
Or blue or sometimes red
When the sun rises or sets,
A hundred shades of overcast—
I rest my eyes on that.

The Survivor

Those bodies now are dead
Which I embraced.
Hanon is gone who promised not to leave me,
And Julian's gone, who was
The soulmate of my youth,
And Lester whom I loved …
And I, for reasons I will never understand,
Am chosen by God? by destiny?
By random chance? to play
The sad survivor of those loves, to live
Without love in an empty world.
And wonder why I who am weak
Am fated to survive the strong
And good. Does this fate
Carry some obligation?

First Step

So many years since you left me,
And painfully I survive without you.
And now I am ready to take the path
That you mapped out in a prison cell
In Belo Horizonte. Now
I am ready to take the first step
On the path of that map.

At last, dear Julian, we move
Together towards the goal.

THE BIRD FLIES

The bird flies because it knows
It will not fall.
When I say "I know," I know
What I mean.
But when I say "The bird knows,"
It is hard to define
What "know" means.

In the end when it dies
It will lie on the ground
Or sink into the water,
But while it lives it flies
Because it knows
That it can fly.

I Grieve

Instead of being grateful
For what I have
I grieve for what I have lost.

Time

The silence of time
And its roar
As it twirls by
Is as unthinkable
As it is unmeasurable
Because we have no standard
By which to measure it.
A day. A lifetime. A light year.
A dark year. The poets and philosophers
All have their try at a definition,
This is this, that is that,
And eventually all shrug it off
As inconceivable.
And so I watch my last hours
Go by on a little clock
That used to go round and round
But now only flashes numbers.

Watching the Sky

The sky is good to watch.
It holds the air
Through which sometimes birds fly.
It holds the promise of infinity
Or the curvature of space.
It holds the clouds that ever change.
It holds the stars, the sun,
The darkness and the light.
It rests the eyes.

Faithful Practice

Living in a land
That's had the wit to elect
A not-altogether-white president
(I didn't vote for him,
I'm an Anarchist)
And then denigrate him
(Note the word denigrate:
Parse it.)
I sometimes despair
That my art won't be enough
To get anyone out of the muck.
But I practice it faithfully
In the hope
That it might.

The Bird

Before the night is over
I will have dreamed your dream.
The wide wingspread of the Bird
Opens above me. The air is colder below.
We will never know what it means,
Not having been given the language
To contain it. The scientist probes
The truth with innocent fingers.
Her mind is silenced by the ignorance
Of her imaginings. "Nothing is free,"
Says the Bird. But what does the Bird know
Of the vastness of the air above it?
Of the weight that it causes?
The air comforts her. The Bird
Lifts her towards the crack of dawn.
The crack widens slowly.
The night is large, says the Bird.
The day is narrow, she answers.

JUSTICE

I have been rewarded
For all the good I have done,
But O God how
I have been punished
For all the good I failed to do
That I should have done.

Tides

Wading between the high tide
And the low tide, the water
ankle deep or knee high ...
What do we learn from the tides
But that the high recedes
And the low fulfills?
Is that true? Is that what we learn
From the high tide and the low tide,
Or is it all an illusion,
Ankle deep and knee high?

Weaving

Weaving the mind's eye
To separate the essential
From the superfluous,
We stumble over the detritus
Of a process of weeding
And wonder if there is something
To be learned there in the heap
Of what has been eliminated.
Yes, there is. Let us study.

Discourse

The silence slides between their words
Like a buttery substance. "What do you mean?"
She asks. "What do you mean?" he answers.
And the great gulf between one and one
Is never breached, nor healed, nor understood.

The creature of the night
And the creature of the day
Are both present in the twilight
And the dawn. But they can never meet.

So they greet each other
By their separate names,
And hope some gap is closed.
"What do you mean?" she asks.

As If

A few more words
Before the endless silence

Concerned with the richness
And ripeness
Of the moment

Leaving no gap in the experience
But living it
Through and through

As if it were true

Now That I Am Home

Now that I am home
And I know there is nowhere else to go
And because I know what death is,
I know we'll not meet again.
Should I be satisfied
That I know my fate
Or despair that it's so dismal?

Still I must make peace
With what I am now
If I am to help make peace
In the world. As if there were
No distinction between myself
And the world.
As if there were no distinction
Between the world and its dismal fate.

Sunset

Sunset takes place for me
Behind a twelve-story building
On Suffolk Street.
The dimensions of the Lower East Side
Are perfectly aligned
To the dimensions
Of the solar system
And of the galaxies, all of which
Are contained on the Lower East Side
Or wherever it is
That you experience the sunset
When you come home.

No, No, No, No, No

In my decrepitude
I like to imagine
That I will yet grow strong
And dance again

And I ask myself
Wouldn't it be better
To abandon such hopes
And let myself realize
That I am growing weaker?

No, No, No, No, No.
I will yet grow strong
And dance again.

All the Way

Having gone all the way,
And seeing that it is nothing,
She yawned on her bed of resignation
And smiled at the sky, and she said,
"Remember me."

Having finally gone all the way,
And realizing that it had no meaning
To excel, to win, to be the very first,
She looked down at the earth
And prayed toward what she no longer believed.

And slept.

And in that sleep she dreamt
Of what could be, but what was not.
And optimism dueled with pessimism,
And won.

And so she woke
And started all over again.

Hard Lessons

Learn patience first,
And after patience, love,
And after love
The eternal joy
Of having loved.

www.ingramcontent.com/pod-product-compliance
Lightning Source LLC
Chambersburg PA
CBHW030050100426
42734CB00038B/998